Jesus + Me

Talking with My Greatest Friend

Melissa Kirking

ASCENSION
Kids

Introduction for Parents

Children need guidance when they are learning any new skills. It is the same with learning how to spend time with Jesus, their "Divine Friend," their best friend, their friend who is God.[1] It is good for children to learn how to guide themselves in prayer. We want to foster a craving within the children to spend time conversing with God.

The purpose of this prayer book, *Jesus and Me*, is to help children guide themselves through heartfelt, profound time with their Divine Friend. This book incorporates a wide variety of prayers, styles, and methods that will draw children closer to Jesus. This prayer book equips children with a clear step-by-step blueprint for a meaningful conversation with our Lord. It leads children through some basic forms of prayer in the life of a follower of Jesus: praise, contrition, thanksgiving, and petitions (intercessions). It also reminds children to take some necessary quiet time to listen to Jesus, gives additional prayer possibilities if their prayer time allows, and prompts children to say their goodbyes to Jesus when they are finished.

The variety of prayers will help children to develop and maintain a strong, genuine, unmistakable, and eternal friendship with Jesus. This book allows children to pick and choose the prayers that appeal to them in that moment in time. Yet it also broadens the children's prayer base by stretching and encouraging them to try new methods of praying. It allows children to focus on Jesus without needing to wonder what to do during their conversation with him.

In addition, *Jesus and Me* introduces children to the language of their Catholic Faith and the wisdom of saints and popes, and it encourages children to actively live and learn their faith outside of their prayer time in their daily lives. This prayer book is a tool to open wider the door to a deeper friendship with God and our Catholic Faith.

Jesus and Me supplies children with the means and flexibility to experience a pleasant time of prayer with their Divine Friend. It reinforces the importance of spending time with the One who loves them most. Children will develop a deep and personal relationship with Jesus, who will guide them through their entire lives. This time with Jesus flows forth into their daily lives and teaches them to turn to him often. How wonderful to develop this relationship early in life — a relationship that will hold them close to Jesus in their youth and adult years!

CONTENTS

Who Is Jesus?

God

Born to Mary and Joseph
on Christmas Day

Second Person of
the Holy Trinity

True God and
true Man

Divine Friend

The Eucharist

Always loving

Best friend

Ever forgiving

Rose from the dead
on Easter Sunday

Full of endless mercy

Died for my sins
on Good Friday

HOW TO USE THIS BOOK

"Why should I use this book?"

Jesus is your Divine Friend! You want to talk to him! You want to spend time with him! You want to pray! But sometimes you might not know how or what to say.

This book helps you with the "how." This book gives you many, many ways to spend time with Jesus and guides you to use all four kinds of prayer:

praise	being sorry
thanksgiving	asking Jesus

plus some bonus **pray more** possibilities

"Where should I use this book?"

Anywhere you go to pray can be your prayer space, so you can use this book anywhere:

- at home
- sitting outside
- waiting for Mass to begin
- in Adoration, where you sit before Jesus in the Eucharist

"How should I use this book?"

YOUR GOAL:

Pick and pray one of each of the four kinds of prayer during your prayer time: **praise, being sorry, thanksgiving,** and **asking Jesus.**

- You pick the prayers!

- No need to go in order.

- Choose a new prayer possibility.

- Or choose a prayer possibility you already used.

- Take time to try every prayer in this book.

- And then use all the prayers over and over again!

Many of the prayer prompts in this book will ask you to journal, which means writing down or drawing your thoughts, ideas, and hopes.

No one will grade what you write and draw, so there is no need to be perfect.

Just write and draw what is in your heart and soul as a way for you to get closer to Jesus.

It would be helpful to bring a journal, notebook, or sketchbook along with your favorite pencil or pen with you to your prayer space.

What Is Prayer?
Talking with Your Divine Friend

Jesus is **THE** most amazing friend you could ever have. He is your Divine Friend,[2] your friend from heaven, your friend who is God!

Jesus is always waiting to help you, guide you, talk to you, and listen to you. He is never too busy for you.

> Jesus wants you to share your worries and your joys with him. In fact, he wants to share everything with you!

When you are with your human friends, you spend time talking and listening to each other. Sometimes you might even just spend time together quietly side by side. Since you enjoy each other's company, you get excited for the next visit with your friends.

Spending time together also helps you learn how to trust your friends. Talking, listening, and being with someone is how your friendships grow stronger and closer.

It is the same with your Divine Friend, Jesus! You need to spend time with Jesus. It's so important!

Talking and listening to Jesus is PRAYER.

The more time you spend talking with Jesus and listening to him, the closer and stronger your friendship with your Divine Friend will become.

Prayer is how you come to trust Jesus more and more with your mind, your heart, and your soul.

How can you spend time with Jesus? **Prayer!**

How can you tell Jesus he is wonderful? **Prayer!**

How can you share your day with Jesus? **Prayer!**

How can you hear Jesus speak? **Prayer!**

How can you ask Jesus for help? **Prayer!**

How can you tell Jesus you are sorry for hurting him? **Prayer!**

How can you get to know Jesus better? **Prayer!**

How can you learn to trust Jesus? **Prayer!**

There is even a special time of prayer called ADORATION you can try. This is when you sit in the same room as Jesus in the Eucharist. If you are curious to learn more about Adoration, turn to the back of this book.

Types of Prayer
Conversations with Jesus

In a good friendship, you and your friend talk to each other often and enjoy being together. Sometimes you just share what is going on in your life.

Other times you talk to your friend for certain reasons. And of course, you take time to listen to what your friend has to say.

Your Divine Friend, Jesus, wants a great, strong friendship with you, too!

This amazing friend, God, helps you at all moments in your life, comforts you when no one else is around, listens to you always, and loves to talk to you about anything.

He gives you strength when you need it. He knows the best choices for you to make, forgives completely when you offend him, and leads you to ultimate happiness in heaven.

Jesus wants you to talk to him often! And he has wonderful things to say to you, too, if you take the time to listen.

Just like you talk to your earthly friends for certain reasons, there are four basic ways to pray to your Divine Friend, Jesus.

These conversations or prayers are

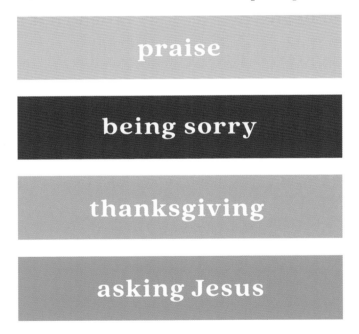

praise

being sorry

thanksgiving

asking Jesus

Think about when you use these types of prayers in your conversations with Jesus. Then you can turn to the matching prayer section of the book to learn more.

In addition to these ways of talking to friends, you pause so your friend can talk. You pay attention and listen to their words.

Jesus, your Divine Friend, wants to talk to you, too, so it is important to pause, be quiet, and listen.

He wants to let you know you are loved.

He might want you to do something.
Or he might have help for your worries.

Hearing Jesus speak is different from hearing an earthly friend speak.

It is very, very, very rare to hear Jesus speak to you in a regular human voice. But Jesus speaks to you in so many other ways!

HOW DO I LISTEN TO JESUS?

Still your body.

Close your eyes.

Slow your breathing.

Then, you clear your mind, putting your day-to-day thoughts out of your mind. As if using a broom, sweep your mind clear so you focus only on God.

While you are listening, if thoughts of school, games, what you will do later, or anything else pop into your mind, again sweep the thoughts away with the broom so you focus only on God. Or, you can talk about that thought with God.

When your mind and heart are focused on God, he can speak to you and you can listen.

Just BE with God.

Jesus can talk to you in the quiet of your heart.

This is why you need to be quiet to hear him.

Jesus always talks to you through Scripture (the Bible).

The Scriptures are God's Word.

Jesus may also speak to you with a strong feeling that you should do something.

His voice may sound like a thought that keeps going through your mind.

Sometimes, he talks to you when you read or listen to a prayer or hear the homily at Mass.

It may make you light up and think, "Oh!"

Other times, Jesus' words might cause a feeling of peace or love to come over you.

These thoughts, feelings, and answers that come from God speaking to you will ALWAYS lead you closer to God and toward heaven.

They will also lead you to show love for others.

They will always, always lead you away from sin.
(Sins are the ways you offend God by what you do, think, and say.)

Jesus will never tell you to do something that is wrong or goes against the Scriptures and Church teachings.

Jesus would not have you keep a secret from your parents either.

Just like you recognize your friend's voice, you will come to recognize Jesus' voice in the quiet.

Sometimes, you won't hear Jesus speak to you.

That is OK!

But you always need to give Jesus the chance to speak by being quiet and still.

If you are busy with your own thoughts and always talking to him, you don't give him the chance to be heard over you.

OPTIONAL JOURNAL ENTRY:

If you feel Jesus speak to you, write it down in your journal. Sometimes he won't, and that is OK.

LET'S PRAY

1 Look through the sections. Pick out one prayer possibility from each prayer type: praise, **being sorry**, thanksgiving, and asking Jesus. If you don't want to decide ahead of time which ones you will pray, you can choose as you go.

2 Find a quiet spot to talk with your Divine Friend, Jesus. Perhaps your room, church, outside, or at Adoration.

3 Take a moment to tell Jesus hello and that you love him.

4 Turn to your selected prayer possibility in the yellow section: praise.

Fold the book back on itself so you see only that section's prayer possibility.

 Slowly and prayerfully experience your time of friendship with God using that prayer possibility.

 Repeat these steps with your chosen prayer possibility in each of the remaining prayer sections.

At the end of your prayer time, turn to the **Before You Go** section. Prayerfully go through the steps.

NOTES

The traditional order for praying is **praise**, **being sorry**, **thanksgiving**, and **asking Jesus**.

But you don't always have to follow that order.

There might be times when you are really excited about something Jesus has done in your life, so you go straight to the **thanksgiving** section.

Other times, your heart is hurting, so you head right to the **ask Jesus** section to pour out your troubles and ask Jesus for help.

There might even be visits with Jesus where you spend more time talking with him in one prayer section and don't make it to the rest of the sections.

All these ways of talking to your Divine Friend are OK!

WHAT ARE PRAISE PRAYERS?

When you notice great things your friends can do or something neat about them, you give them a compliment.

You might say, "You are a great soccer player!" or "I like your hair."

Your Divine Friend, Jesus, has many great and wonderful things about him!

When you notice these wonderful things and give him a compliment, it is called a praise prayer.

Praise is when you give God glory for just being God, not for what he gives you or does for you.

You use words such as

"Wow, Jesus! You are the most awesome friend!"
or "Jesus, you are Love!"
or "Jesus, you are 'the way, and the truth, and the life'" (John 14:6).

WORDS TO KNOW

DIVINE: one who is God

HYMN: song

PRAISE: worship, compliment, and celebrate

EUCHARIST: Jesus present under the appearance of bread, called a Host, which was consecrated during Mass; the true Body, Blood, Soul, and Divinity of Jesus

SAVIOR: another name for Jesus

SOUL: the spiritual, undying part of you

TRINITY: one God in three persons: the Father, the Son, and the Holy Spirit

PONDER: think and consider prayerfully

MERCY: love, kindness, and forgiveness

PRAISE
Prayer Possibilities

1 Slowly, joyfully, and thoughtfully pray what the choir of angels sings in heaven and what you joyfully sing at Mass:

"Holy, Holy, Holy Lord God of hosts. Heaven and earth are full of your glory."

Bonus activity after your prayer time:

At Mass, listen for the hymn and sing it with joy. Jesus will soon become present in the Host.

2 Slowly, joyfully, and thoughtfully pray:

Praise you, **Lord, while I get ready for school.**

Praise you, **Lord, on my way to school.**

Praise you, **Lord, in the classroom.**

Praise you, **Lord, during math.**

Praise you, **Lord, during reading.**

Praise you, **Lord, during spelling.**

Praise you, **Lord, during science.**

Praise you, **Lord, during social science.**

Praise you, **Lord, during lunchtime.**

Praise you, **Lord, during recess.**

Praise you, **Lord, during library time.**

Praise you, **Lord, while I wait in line.**

Praise you, **Lord, when I play with my friends.**

Praise you, **Lord, on my way home.**

Praise you, **Lord, while I do my homework.**

Bonus activity after your prayer time:

Throughout the week, praise Jesus in all the activities you do.

3 JOURNAL ENTRY:

Write "WOW" in bubble letters in your journal.

Fill in the WOW with praise words,
descriptions, or names of Jesus.

(You can use the word bank on the next page to help you.)

Bonus activity after your prayer time:

Share with a family member some of your favorite
words you used to describe Jesus as **WOW**.

WORD BANK:

my God

my Savior

my King

my Lord

my Creator

my hiding place

my nourishment

my everything

my Divine Friend

my judge

the Rock

protector
of my soul

the One who loves
me the most

THE miracle
of miracles
(the Eucharist)

Light of the World

the Way

the Truth

giver of life

son of Mary

Son of the Father

second Person of
the Trinity

giver of peace

Lord on high

everlasting life

Creator of all

a treasure

always the same

awe-inspiring

wondrous

generous

awesome

faithful

mighty

holy

miraculous

love

joy

peace

magnificent

amazing

patient

powerful

fantastic

the Light

Bread of
Heaven

4 Slowly, joyfully, and thoughtfully pray the Divine Praises. (The Divine Praises are a set of prayers normally said at the end of a group Eucharistic Adoration).

"Blessed be **God.**

Blessed be **his holy Name.**

Blessed be **Jesus Christ, true God and true Man.**

Blessed be **the name of Jesus.**

Blessed be **his most Sacred Heart.**

Blessed be **his most Precious Blood.**

Blessed be **Jesus in the most holy Sacrament of the altar.**

Blessed be **the Holy Spirit, the Paraclete.**

Blessed be **the great Mother of God, Mary most holy.**

Blessed be **her holy and Immaculate Conception.**

Blessed be **her glorious Assumption.**

Blessed be **the name of Mary, Virgin and Mother.**

Blessed be **St. Joseph, her most chaste spouse.**

Blessed be **God in his angels and in his saints."**

(The most holy Sacrament of the altar is another name for the Eucharist.

Paraclete is another name for the Holy Spirit.

The Immaculate Conception describes how the Blessed Mother came into the world without sin.

The Assumption was when the Blessed Mother's body and soul were taken to heaven at the end of her life.)

5 Slowly, joyfully, and thoughtfully pray this prayer.
You may go through all the praises or pick your favorites.

Jesus, you are my God. I adore you!

Jesus, you are my Savior. I adore you!

Jesus, you are my King. I adore you!

Jesus, you are my Lord. I adore you!

Jesus, you are the giver of life. I adore you!

Jesus, you are my Creator. I adore you!

Jesus, you are my hiding place. I adore you!

Jesus, you are the protector of my soul. I adore you!

Jesus, you are my nourishment. I adore you!

Jesus, you are my everything. I adore you!

Jesus, you are a treasure. I adore you!

Jesus, you are always the same. I adore you!

Jesus, you are awe-inspiring. I adore you!

Jesus, you are wondrous. I adore you!

Jesus, you are generous. I adore you!

Jesus, you are awesome. I adore you!

Jesus, you are faithful. I adore you!

Jesus, you are mighty. I adore you!

Jesus, you are miraculous. I adore you!

Jesus, you are love. I adore you!

Jesus, you are magnificent. I adore you!

Jesus, you are amazing. I adore you!

Jesus, you are unchangeable. I adore you!

Jesus, you are just. I adore you!

Jesus, you are patient. I adore you!

Jesus, you are tender. I adore you!

Jesus, you are approachable. I adore you!

Jesus, you are constant. I adore you!

Jesus, you are breathtaking. I adore you!

Jesus, you are merciful. I adore you!

Jesus, you are sovereign (the King). I adore you!

Jesus, you are peace. I adore you!

Jesus, you are powerful. I adore you!

Jesus, you are joy. I adore you!

Jesus, you are brilliant. I adore you!

Jesus, you are fantastic. I adore you!

6 Slowly, joyfully, and thoughtfully pray Daniel 3:29–30:

"Blessed are you, O Lord, the God of our fathers,

and to be praised and highly exalted for ever;

And blessed is your glorious holy name

and to be highly praised and highly exalted for ever."

Ponder:

Jesus' name is holy and glorious.
Is his name special?
Why is "Jesus" a glorious name?

7 Our duty is to praise Jesus. (A duty is a job or responsibility.) Ponder the words of St. John Paul II:

" 'My soul give thanks to the Lord … give thanks to the Lord *and never forget all his blessings*' (Ps. 103(102), 1-2).

"This is a task for each human being. Only the human person, created in the image and likeness of God, is capable of raising a hymn of praise and thanksgiving to the Creator. The earth, with all its creatures, and the entire universe, call on man to be their voice. Only the human person is capable of releasing from the depths of his or her being that hymn of praise, proclaimed without words by all creation: 'My soul, give thanks to the Lord; all my being, bless his holy name' (Ps. 103(102), 1)."[3]

Slowly, joyfully, and thoughtfully pray:

"My soul, give thanks to the Lord; all my being, bless his holy name."

Bonus activity after your prayer time:

When something wonderful happens at school or home, say aloud or silently in your mind, "My soul, give thanks to the Lord; all my being, bless his holy name."

8 JOURNAL ENTRY:

Write the letters for JESUS in your journal, one under each other.

Write words to describe Jesus that begin with each letter. See the example below.

J – jaw dropping

E – encouraging

S – safe

U – unblemished

S – soothing

9 Slowly, joyfully, thoughtfully pray:

I praise you, Jesus, **when I am happy.**

I praise you, Jesus, **when I am sad.**

I praise you, Jesus, **when I am hurt.**

I praise you, Jesus, **when I am confused.**

I praise you, Jesus, **when I am excited.**

I praise you, Jesus, **when I am scared.**

I praise you, Jesus, **when I am worried.**

I praise you, Jesus, **when I am peaceful.**

I praise you, Jesus, **when I am silly.**

I praise you, Jesus, **when I am awake.**

I praise you, Jesus, **when I am busy.**

I praise you, Jesus, **when I am bored.**

I praise you, Jesus, **when I am running.**

I praise you, Jesus, **when I am walking.**

I praise you, Jesus, **when I am standing.**

I praise you, Jesus, **when I am sitting.**

I praise you, Jesus, **always!**

Bonus activity after your prayer time:

Throughout the week, praise Jesus no matter how you are feeling, especially when you are sad, hurt, angry, or worried.

10 Slowly, joyfully, thoughtfully pray:

Prayer in Praise of God by St. Francis of Assisi

"You are holy, Lord, the only God,

And Your deeds are wonderful.

You are strong.

You are great.

You are the Most High.

You are Almighty.

You, Holy Father, are King of heaven and earth.

You are Three and One, Lord God, all Good.

You are Good, all Good, supreme Good,

Lord God, living and true.

You are love. You are wisdom.

You are humility.

You are endurance.

You are rest.

You are peace.

You are joy and gladness.

You are justice and moderation.

You are all our riches, and You suffice for us.

You are beauty.

You are gentleness.

You are our protector.

You are our guardian and defender.

You are our courage.

You are our haven and our hope.

You are our faith, our great consolation.

You are our eternal life, Great and Wonderful Lord, God Almighty, Merciful Savior."[4]

11 JOURNAL ENTRY:

Write "Jesus you are:" in large letters in the middle of your journal page.

Creatively write some or all of the following words around **"Jesus you are"** with fancy lettering, swirls, patterns, and simple drawings.

As you write the word, ponder the meaning.

- my God
- my Divine Friend
- son of Mary
- Son of the Father
- Lord on high
- the One who loves me the most
- the Bread of Life

- everlasting life
- Creator of all
- Light of the world
- second Person of the Trinity
- giver of peace
- my judge
- my hiding place

- the Way
- the Truth
- Savior
- Rock
- love
- holy
- joy
- amazing

See the example below.

my Divine
Friend

JESUS YOU ARE

joy

the Way
the Truth

12 JOURNAL ENTRY:

Write Psalm 9:1–2 in your journal and
then joyfully pray it to Jesus:

"I will tell of all your wonderful deeds.

I will be glad and exult in you,

I will sing praise to your name, O Most High."

13 JOURNAL ENTRY:

Write:

Jesus you are

A

M

A

Z

I

N

G

Then write praise words about Jesus starting with the letter on each line.

Praise words are words that show you worship, compliment, and celebrate Jesus.

14 Slowly, joyfully, and thoughtfully pray three times:

You are my Creator!

My greatest treasure,

the source of my joy,

the giver of love.

Bonus activity after your prayer time:

Slowly, joyfully, and thoughtfully pray this prayer one extra time during the week.

15 JOURNAL ENTRY:

Write Psalm 145:21 in your journal and then joyfully pray it to Jesus:

"My mouth will speak the praises of the Lord."

Bonus activity after your prayer time:
Let your mouth speak a praise of Jesus to a friend.

16 Slowly, joyfully, and thoughtfully pray the following prayer.

After each line, close your eyes to ponder
and picture the image in your mind.

God, you are like a candle on a moonless night,
shining brightly in the dark. Praise you, Jesus!

God, you are like a giant oak tree,
tall and majestic. Praise you, Jesus!

God, you are like a warm, cozy blanket, surrounding
and comforting me. Praise you, Jesus!

God, you are like crashing waves at the beach,
strong and powerful. Praise you, Jesus!

God, you are like my favorite stuffed animal that,
when I was younger, I could hold tight to when I was
scared so that I could be brave. Praise you, Jesus!

God, you are like a speeding jet plane,
quick to reach me. Praise you, Jesus!

God, you are like a road map, guiding me on
my journey through life to heaven. Praise you, Jesus!

God, you are like a doctor, covering and
healing my wounds. Praise you, Jesus!

God, you are like blue skies,
stretching beyond my view. Praise you, Jesus!

God, you are like an amazing sunset,
spreading beauty in my world. Praise you, Jesus!

God, you are like a fire truck, rushing to help
people in danger. Praise you, Jesus!

God, you are *the* Bread who gives me life.
Praise you, Jesus!

17 JOURNAL ENTRY:

Write Psalm 95:2–3 in your journal and
then joyfully pray it to Jesus:

"Let us come into his presence with thanksgiving;

    let us make a joyful noise to him with songs of praise!

For the LORD is a great God,

    and a great King above all gods."

Silently sing a song of praise to Jesus in your mind. You
can sing one that you already know or make up your own.

Optional journal entry:
In your journal, write down the words of your song.

Bonus activity after your prayer time:
Sing your song of praise to Jesus again and again.

18 Slowly, joyfully, and thoughtfully pray
Daniel 3:33–34:

"Blessed are you upon the throne of your kingdom
and to be extolled and highly exalted for ever.
Blessed are you in the firmament of heaven
and to be sung and glorified for ever."

JOURNAL ENTRY

Draw Jesus on his heavenly throne and yourself kneeling down in praise in front of him.

Being exalted and glorified means God is worshipped and known as kingly, marvelous, and great.

19

Slowly, joyfully, and thoughtfully pray Daniel 3:57–60, 3:68. As you pray, think of all the creatures within each line. Imagine those creatures praising the Lord.

Optional journal entry:

Draw a picture of different creatures or people praising the Lord.

"Bless the Lord, you whales and all creatures
that move in the waters,
    sing praise to him and highly exalt him for ever"

... whales, goldfish, crabs, shrimp, clams ...

"Bless the Lord, all birds of the air,
    sing praise to him and highly exalt him for ever"

... cardinals, hawks, robins, woodpeckers ...

"Bless the Lord, all beasts and cattle,
    sing praise to him and highly exalt him for ever"

... dogs, cats, tigers, worms, cheetahs ...

"Bless the Lord, you sons of men [that is, humans],
    sing praise to him and highly exalt him for ever"

... grandmas, police officers, teachers, sisters ...

"Bless him, all who worship the Lord, the God of gods,
    sing praise to him and give thanks to him,
    for his mercy endures for ever."

20 Slowly, joyfully, and thoughtfully pray:

Jesus,

I treasure you!

I adore you!

I stand in awe of you!

I hope in you!

I love you!

I trust you!

Bonus activity after your prayer time:

Slowly, joyfully, and thoughtfully pray this prayer one extra time during the week.

WHAT ARE *BEING* SORRY PRAYERS?

When you hurt your friend's feelings or body, it is important to tell your friend you are sorry. You hurt your Divine Friend sometimes, too, with your sins.

Sins are the ways people offend God by what they do, think, and say.

When you tell Jesus you are sorry, you are saying a **being sorry prayer**, also known as a prayer of contrition.

You apologize to God with all your heart for offending him. Part of a **being sorry prayer** is asking Jesus to forgive you.

Jesus has so much love for you that you can trust that he will always forgive you.

You just need to be sorry from your heart. You also need to try hard not to repeat the sin because you love God so much you don't want to offend him again.[5]

The Catholic Church has a special sacrament called Reconciliation, also known as the sacrament of Penance and confession.

In the sacrament of Reconciliation, you go to a priest to tell him your sins and are forgiven by God.

WORDS TO KNOW:

SIN: the ways you offend God by what you do, think and say

RECONCILIATION: the sacrament when you go to a priest to tell him your sins and are forgiven by God; also called Penance and confession

OFFEND: do wrong, fail to do good

GRACE: "the *free and undeserved help* that God gives us to respond to his call to become children of God" (*Catechism of the Catholic Church* 1996)

PONDER: think and consider prayerfully

CONTRITION: being sorry

BEING SORRY

Prayer Possibilities

1 Sometimes you offend God by your actions, thoughts, and words.

In your heart, answer the following questions as an examination of conscience to guide your thoughts as to how you may have offended Jesus.

(An examination of conscience is when, with God's help, you think of any sins you may have committed.)

- Have I said mean things or hurt someone's feelings?
- Am I jealous of anyone, or do I wish bad things on someone?
- Do I listen to my parents and teachers?
- Do I help out when needed?
- Have I been saying my prayers?
- Do I trust in God at all times?
- Do I give God enough attention?
- Do I live my life the way Jesus wants me to?

If needed, ask Jesus for forgiveness and ask your parents to help you find a time to go to Reconciliation.

2 As you slowly and thoughtfully pray, think about any sins you may have committed:

"Oh Lord, forgive me my sins. I love you and I wish to love you for all eternity! Let this sacrament wipe out all the sins I have ever committed by

my eyes,

my ears,

my lips and

my feet:

may my soul and body be made holy by the merits of your Sacred Passion."[6]

— St. Dominic Savio

Tell Jesus any sins you committed with your eyes, your ears, your lips, and your feet.

If needed, ask Jesus for forgiveness and ask your parents to help you find a time to go to Reconciliation.

3 Jesus is always, always willing to help you or anyone else in need. He is immensely kind and so very, very loving.

Jesus loves us in a way that is so much bigger than the way a human person can love. He loves people even when they offend him with their sins.

He is always ready to forgive us.

This is Jesus' divine mercy. Jesus' divine mercy is enormous. It is so much bigger than you can possibly understand.

Optional journal entry:

Draw yourself swimming in the oceans of Jesus' mercy.

Read this prompt, and close your eyes after each line or two.
Use your imagination to picture what you read in your mind.

Picture oceans of Jesus' mercy with no end in sight.

Imagine that Jesus' mercy is so large you can swim through
it. As you swim through his ocean of mercy, it feels amazing.
You feel love surround your entire body and fill your heart.

Jesus' mercy cleanses you and makes you pure as you
swim through it.

His love and mercy are so incredible that Jesus forgives
your wrongdoings as long as you are truly sorry.

Jesus' mercy removes any sins that are stuck on you like

barnacles holding onto the side of a whale.

Jesus' mercy is so miraculously huge that others can be
in his ocean of mercy at the same time as you.

In Jesus' oceans of mercy, you find love, forgiveness,
blessings, and strength.

Spend a few moments talking to Jesus about his oceans
of divine mercy.

4 Sometimes it is hard to admit you've done something sinful. You might pretend you did not sin, you might try to give excuses as to why the sin is not your fault, or you might just pay no attention to it.

Pope Francis suggests:

"Let us ask for the grace to live in the truth without hiding anything from the Lord and without hiding anything from ourselves."[7]

Ask Jesus to show you any sins you may have committed so you can see the sin. Then, ask Jesus for forgiveness.

5 JOURNAL ENTRY:

Ponder the words of Pope Francis:

"We too, with the Lord, should have the freedom to say things as they are: 'Lord, I am in sin, help me.' "[8]

Write your sins in your journal to prepare for Reconciliation.
Ask Jesus to help you to do better and to stop sinning.

Bonus activity after your prayer time:

When you feel the temptation to sin, say to Jesus, "Lord, help me. I don't want to sin."

6 Ponder Pope Francis' words:

"An Act of Contrition, made well. In this way our souls will become as white as snow."[9]

Act of Contrition

"My God, I am sorry for my sins with all my heart. In choosing to do wrong and failing to do good, I have sinned against you whom I should love above all things. I firmly intend, with your help, to do penance, to sin no more, and to avoid whatever leads me to sin. Our Savior Jesus Christ suffered and died for us. In his name, my God, have mercy."

Close your eyes and imagine your sins as messy smudges on your soul. Imagine Jesus making your soul as white and as pure as snow.

7 As you slowly and thoughtfully pray, think about any sins you have committed:

Lord, guide me today to see my sins,

obvious sins and hidden sins,

sins that were seen by other people and

sins that I committed in my heart and mind.

Sins offend you, your mother, and other people.

Lord, please help me to make a good confession.

Lord, please help me to scrub my soul clean.

Now slowly wipe down your arms, chest, and legs like you are cleaning dirt off of you. With each wipe, ask Jesus to scrub your soul clean from sin.

If needed, ask your parents to help you find a time to go to Reconciliation.

8 Jesus forgives you when you ask him. You need to forgive others as well. Prayerfully ask him,

"Lord, who do I need to forgive?"

Take a few minutes to listen for Jesus' answer.

If he brings someone's name to your mind, ask Jesus to help you forgive that person or those people.

9 St. John Paul II spoke directly to young people in one of his homilies. Ponder his words:

"To all the young people of the Church, I extend a special invitation to receive Christ's forgiveness and his strength in the Sacrament of Penance. It is a *mark of greatness* to be able to say:

I have made a mistake:

I have sinned, Father;

I am sorry; I ask for pardon;

I will try again, because

I rely on your strength and

I believe in your love.

Bonus activity after your prayer time:

After your prayer time, talk with your parents about when you can "receive Christ's forgiveness and his strength in the Sacrament of Penance."

And I know that the power of your Son's Paschal Mystery – the Death and Resurrection of our Lord Jesus Christ – is *greater than my weaknesses and all the sins of the world*. I will come and confess my sins and be healed, and I will live in your love!"[10]

Remember, the sacrament of Penance is the sacrament when you go to a priest to tell him your sins and get forgiveness from God.

10

Read the words of Scripture:

"Holy is his name" (Luke 1:49).

And,

"At the name of Jesus every knee should bow, in heaven and on earth and under the earth, and every tongue confess that Jesus Christ is Lord, to the glory of God the Father" (Philippians 2:10–11).

Bonus activity after your prayer time:

At Mass or in Adoration, look at Jesus in the Blessed Sacrament. Pray, "Jesus, you are Lord! Jesus, you are God!" Tell him that you know it is true.

Jesus' name is holy!

You should always be loving and respectful
when you say "Jesus" or "God" or "Jesus Christ."

Think about the way you speak Jesus' name.

Do you speak "Jesus"
or "God" or "Jesus
Christ" with love?

With reverence
(that means, with
deep respect)?

Or do you use "Jesus"
or "God" when you
are frustrated,
surprised, or mad?

Do you use his
holy name like
a swear word?

Do you need to make any changes? If you do, ask Jesus to help
you honor him better and to treat his name with reverence.

11 Pope Francis helped people ponder the usefulness of doing an examination of conscience at the end of every day.[11] An examination of conscience is when, with God's help, you think of any sins you may have committed.

These are some questions that you can use to help look at the choices you have made.

As you think about your day,

- **Remember when you felt like sinning.**

- **Remember the times you actually did sin.**

- **Remember the times that you avoided sinning with the help of the Holy Spirit.**

Basically, when you think about your day with an eye on how you were tempted to sin, how you did sin, and how you resisted sin, you can know "what is going on in the heart."

Understanding what happens in your heart is important in your journey to life in heaven with Jesus.

"May the Lord teach us to make an examination of conscience every day."

Slowly and thoughtfully answer these questions to help you think about how you may have sinned:[12]

Do I only turn to God when I'm in need?

Do I go to Mass on Sunday and the other days when I must go to Mass (called holy days of obligation)?

Do I take time to pray?

Am I embarrassed to show that I am a Christian?

Do I resist God's will?

Do I forgive my neighbors, friends, and family?

Am I envious?

Am I hot-tempered?

Am I honest with everyone?

Have I led others to do bad things?

Do I honor and respect my parents?

Am I lazy?

Do I want people to serve me?

Do I do things to get back at people or hold grudges?

Am I humble?

If needed, ask Jesus for forgiveness and ask your parents to help you find a time to go to Reconciliation.

12 Think about a time that you got a cut, a bruise, or a bump. These injuries hurt your body, right? **Ponder Jesus' body hurting on the Cross.**

Consider that even though Jesus is God and he could have stopped his body from hurting, he allowed himself to feel the hurt on the Cross.

Jesus hurt because he loves us so very, very much.

You will have different times in life when you will get hurt. With these hurts, you can take a moment to tell Jesus, "I love you. I offer this hurt up to you so you don't have as much hurt."

Offering your hurt up to Jesus is one way you can love Jesus because you are willing to share some of his hurt.

Jesus died on the Cross for the forgiveness of our sins so that we can join him in heaven one day.

Think about any sins you may have committed, especially those that may have hurt another person's body or mind.

Know that sin is a choice to do or not do something.

If you accidentally bump someone, and the person falls and gets hurt, that is not a sin. But it is still polite to apologize to the person.

If needed, ask Jesus for forgiveness and ask your parents to help you find a time to go to Reconciliation.

Optional journal entry:

In your journal, draw Jesus on the Cross.

Bonus activity after your prayer time:

The next time you get hurt, offer it up to Jesus. Say the prayer, "Jesus, I love you. I offer this hurt up to you."

13 Think about a time your body was sick. You may have had to take medicine to get better.

St. Thomas Aquinas says that the same is true with your soul. Your soul can become sick with sin.

The medicine needed for your soul to get better is the graces God gives you in the sacrament of Reconciliation.[13]

Take a few minutes to examine (that is, carefully look at) your soul like a doctor examines your body.

Look for sins that might be making your soul feel sick.

Bonus activity after your prayer time:

Talk with your parents about anything you might be unsure about. If needed, ask your parents to help you find a time to go to Reconciliation.

Think about if you need to find the time to go to the sacrament of Reconciliation for the medicine of God's graces.

14

The *Catechism of the Catholic Church*, a book that explains the details of your Catholic faith, states that asking forgiveness from God for your sins is an important start for good prayer (CCC 2631).

Take a prayerful moment to look in your heart to see if you have offended God in some way through your thoughts, words, or actions.

If needed, ask Jesus for forgiveness and ask your parents to help you find a time to go to Reconciliation.

15 JOURNAL ENTRY:

Write Psalm 103:12 in your journal. Draw a picture to go with the words as you ponder them.

"As far as the east is from the west, so far does he remove our transgressions from us."

(Transgressions are sins.)

16 Ponder Pope Francis' words:

"Gossip can also kill, because it kills the reputation of the person! It is so terrible to gossip! At first it may seem like a nice thing, even amusing, like enjoying a candy. But in the end, it fills the heart with bitterness, and even poisons us."[14]

Gossip is unkind talk about other people without them around. A person's reputation is what others think of them.

Honestly look at your actions. Do you gossip?

If you have gossiped, ask Jesus to forgive you. Ask Jesus for his help to stop gossiping and the courage to say something kind instead.

If needed, ask your parents to help you find a time to go to Reconciliation.

"Confession is an act of honesty and courage; an act of entrusting ourselves, beyond sin, to the mercy of a loving and forgiving God."[15]

— St. John Paul II

17

Jesus wants you to trust him and to have the courage to tell him your sins.

He wants to forgive you!

It can be hard to admit when you have done something wrong, but Jesus' love and forgiveness are larger than the largest thing you can imagine.

Slowly and thoughtfully pray:

**Lord Jesus, Son of God,
have mercy on me, a sinner.
I trust in your love for me.**

Bonus activity after your prayer time:

Any time you realize you have sinned, tell Jesus,

*"Help me. Lord Jesus, Son of God, have mercy on me,
a sinner. I trust in your love for me."*

When needed, ask your parents to help you find a time
to go to the sacrament of Reconciliation.

18 Slowly and thoughtfully read Colossians 3:12–13:

Know you are chosen by God.

You are one of God's holy and beloved chosen ones.

"Put on then, as God's chosen ones, holy and beloved, compassion, kindness, lowliness, meekness, and patience, forbearing one another and, if one has a complaint against another, forgiving each other; as the Lord has forgiven you, so you also must forgive."

> Imagine putting on each one of God's blessings you read about as if each one was a piece of clothing.

Each of these blessings helps you love others more like Jesus loves.

Put on heartfelt compassion.
   (**Compassion means feeling sadness for someone's suffering or sadness and wanting to help the person feel better.**)

Put on kindness.

Put on lowliness.
   (**Lowliness means not thinking too highly of yourself.**)

Put on meekness.
   (**Meekness means accepting God's will.**)

Put on patience.

Put on forgiveness for one another.

If someone has treated you badly or wrongly, ask Jesus to help you forgive that person like he forgives you when you treat him badly or do something wrong against him.

19 St. John Vianney said:

"If we could only see the joy of our Guardian Angel when he sees us fighting our temptations!"[16]

Picture a time you were tempted to sin but did not choose to sin.

Then imagine the happiness on the face of your guardian angel, the angel God specifically asked to help watch over you all your life.

Ask Jesus to help you be strong in times of temptation.

20 Ponder the words of Scripture:

"If we confess our sins, he is faithful and just, and will forgive our sins and cleanse us from all unrighteousness" (1 John 1:9).

Take a prayerful moment to consider any sins you have committed.

Then tell each sin to Jesus one by one.

Tell him you are sorry, and ask him to forgive you.

If needed, ask your parents to help you find a time to go to Reconciliation.

Now close your eyes and allow a feeling of joy to surround you because you fully accept that Jesus is faithful.

This beautiful joy comes from knowing that you never need to be afraid to tell Jesus your sins, because he will always forgive your sins when you are sorry for them.

Bonus activity after your prayer time:
Look up 1 John 1:9 in your Bible and reread it.

WHAT ARE *THANKSGIVING* PRAYERS?

When a friend does something kind for you, you say thank you. When a friend gives you a gift, you say thank you.

Saying thank you lets your friends know that you notice their kindness and appreciate what they have done for you or given to you.

Your Divine Friend, Jesus, gives you many wonderful blessings.

He does countless loving things for you.

It is so important to let him know that you appreciate all that he does. These thank-yous to Jesus are thanksgiving prayers.

WORDS TO KNOW

PONDER: think and consider prayerfully

GRATITUDE: thankfulness

ENDURES: lasts

GLORIFY: praise and worship

HUMILITY: not thinking too highly of yourself

Jesus is so good to you!

He knows better than you do what will
bring you joy and eternal happiness.

THANKSGIVING
Prayer Possibilities

1 Ponder all the good things that God has given you:

- **your parents,**
- **siblings,**
- **friends,**
- **sports,**
- **favorite foods,**
- **the Mass,**
- **the Eucharist,**
- **the way to have everlasting life,**
- **and countless other wonderful blessings.**

Bonus activity after your prayer time:

At bedtime tonight and every night this week, take time to thank Jesus for the blessings and graces he gave you that day.

Silently thank him for each blessing by saying:

"Thank you, Jesus, for _____ and _____."

"Thank you so much, Jesus, for_____ and _____."

In your mind, name each blessing and grace from God that you can think of one by one.

2 JOURNAL ENTRY:

In your journal, make a thanksgiving web like the one below.

Write **"Jesus, thank you"** in the center, and then write the things you are thankful for in bubbles coming off the center.

3 JOURNAL ENTRY:

In your journal, write the letters A to Z under each other like the example below. For each letter, write at least one blessing, person, or item you are thankful for whose name begins with that letter.

A

B

C

Bonus activity after your prayer time:

Use this ABC journal entry again for things you are thankful for. You can use it during Christmas, Lent, Easter, school, vacation, and other times of the year.

4 Jesus heaps blessings upon you. Ponder each of the following categories listed below.

Name specific people or things in each category that you are thankful for. Tell Jesus thank you for each person or item one by one.

Family: name your family members ...

Friends: name your friends ...

Activities: name the activities that you like doing ...

Nature: name the things in nature you like ...

Pets: name your pets or friends' pets you like ...

Things at church: name the things you learn and ways you grow closer to Jesus at church ...

Things at school: name the things you learn and have fun with at school ...

Things that make you happy: name the people, things, and times that make you happy ...

5 Slowly, joyfully, and thoughtfully pray:

God, you are amazing!
You love me with enormous love.
You love me even when I sin.
You always forgive me when I am sorry.
You offer me eternity.
I can always run to you.
You are like a river of mercy, deep and wide.
You bless me.
You created me, the world, and everything everywhere.
You are my rock.
You are where my patience comes from.
You are my compass.
You help me to change in positive ways.
You help me to grow in your love.
You are my God!

6 Count out with your fingers ten or even twenty blessings.

7 Ponder:

God is a master artist.

He designed the entire world and everything in it.

He gave colors, patterns, shapes, and sizes to the

sky, plants, animals, people, and so much more.

Look at the world God designed with the eyes of an artist studying a magnificent painting.

Name all the colors, sizes, shapes, forms, and whatever else your artist eyes see.

Thank Jesus for them.

Now ponder:

God is a master farmer and a master cook.

Name all the amazing foods—fruits, vegetables, meats, side dishes, desserts, and drinks—you have tasted.

Thank Jesus for them.

Bonus activity after your prayer time:

Before you eat lunch at school, in the quiet of your mind tell Jesus thank you for the food.

Say grace:

"Bless us, O Lord, and these, thy gifts, which we are about to receive from thy bounty. Through Christ, our Lord. Amen."

8 So often we ask Jesus for things that we need or want and for the needs of others, but we forget to tell Jesus thank you for those answered prayers, daily blessings, and surprise blessings.

It is important to tell God thank you.

Ponder how you might feel if you gave someone a really nice gift or did something very kind for the person and he or she didn't say thank you.

Think about answered prayers, daily blessings, and surprise blessings that you have forgotten to thank Jesus for. Be sure to say "thank you, Jesus" for each thing you think of.

9   Slowly, joyfully, and thoughtfully pray:

Jesus, your blessings rain down on me like a soft, gentle spring rain shower. You give so many, many more blessings than the raindrops falling from the sky. Your blessings are too many to count. I pay attention to some blessings as they drop on me, and others I don't even think about.

Bonus activity after your prayer time:

Next time it rains, look at all the raindrops falling and think about all the blessings Jesus rains down on you.

With your eyes closed, take two or three minutes to think about Jesus' blessings gently falling on you like raindrops.

Imagine you can feel your body getting covered with warm, gentle, love-filled blessing drops.

10 Tell Jesus:

You, Lord God, are the Creator of all. You create with such beauty, planning, detail, and love.

Ponder the amazingness and variety of creation and thank Jesus for it:

Creator of people:
people who all have emotions, free will, the ability to love like him; people with different talents, skin colors, eye colors, sizes (plump, thin, tall, short)

Creator of plants:
fruits, vegetables, vines, tall trees, dainty flowers, moss, ferns, lily pads, ivy, grass, cactus, herbs, plants with many colors and smells

Creator of animals:
animals that live on land, in the sea, in the air; animals with solid color, stripes, spots, camouflage; animals with long fur, short fur, manes, tails; animals that are tiny, medium-sized, huge; animals with legs, arms, flippers, wings, fins; animals that bark, roar, tweet

Creator of weather:

rain, clouds, thunderstorms, snow, rainbows, storms, sunshine, heat, cold, dry weather, wind, humid weather, fog, mist

Creator of water bodies:

rivers, creeks, ponds, oceans, seas, lakes, glaciers, streams, wetlands, puddles, gulfs, bays, lagoons, harbors, marshes, swamps, bogs, waterfalls, tidal pools

Creator of land formations:

mountains, hills, valleys, plateaus, plains, canyons, peninsulas, volcanoes, beaches, islands, continents, cliffs, caves, deserts, summits

Bonus activity after your prayer time:

Take a nature walk.

Look around at the natural things you pass and give Jesus thanks for each part of his creation you see.

11

Look for joy ...
everywhere,
in everything,
in everyone,
at all times.

Bonus activity after your prayer time:

Spend the next couple of days looking for joy everywhere you go. Ask Jesus to help you have joy in your heart at all times.

12 Ponder this quote:

"No duty is more urgent than that of returning thanks" to God.[17]

Bonus activity after your prayer time:

Work really hard at the job of giving thanks to God for five days.

One of your jobs in life is to give thanks to Jesus.

Have you worked hard at the job of thanksgiving lately?

13 St. Teresa of Calcutta is quoted as saying,

"The best way to show my gratitude to God is to accept everything, even my problems, with joy."

Ponder this prayer in the book of Psalms in the Bible:

"When cares increase within me, your comfort gives me joy." (Psalm 94:19, NABRE)

Prayerfully consider how you can accept even your problems with joy.

Ask Jesus to help you be cheerful when you don't feel like it.

14 JOURNAL ENTRY:

Write Psalm 7:17 in your journal:

"I will give to the LORD the

thanks due to his righteousness,

and I will sing praise to the

name of the LORD, the most high."

Silently sing in your mind a song of thanks to Jesus or use a singing voice to list all that you are thankful for.

Optional journal entry:

In your journal, write down the words of your song.

15 St. Alphonsus Liguori wrote,

"Let us thank God for having called us to His holy faith. It is a great gift, and the number of those who thank God for it is small."

Consider for a moment: What is faith?

Faith is a good habit that only God can place within your soul so that you are able to strongly believe in him.

Faith allows you to believe in all that Jesus taught and the Holy Spirit reveals to be true.

Faith allows you to believe because you know that Jesus is Truth and will not lie.

Bonus activity after your prayer time:

The next time you see a church, take a moment to thank Jesus for the gift of your Catholic faith.

Did you ever consider that faith is a gift?
Ponder if you have ever thanked Jesus for the gift of faith he gave you.

Take time to thank Jesus with all your heart and all your soul for your faith. Now, ask Jesus to make your faith even stronger.

16 Slowly, joyfully, and thoughtfully pray this prayer of thanksgiving that is based on a prayer by St. Gertrude the Great:

Lord God, my Creator, may my soul bless you with all my heart. For the forgiveness of sins, loving Father, I offer you all the sufferings that your beloved Son went through. With great thanksgiving, I adore and bless you because you give us love that is so great it cannot be described. Thank you, Father of all mercy.[18]

17   St. Josemaria Escriva wrote,

"Get used to lifting your heart to God, in acts of thanksgiving, many times a day ... Thank him for everything, because everything is good."[19]

The heart not only means your beating heart in your body but also where you hold and feel love.

Close your eyes. Imagine gathering giant heaps of your love in your hands.

Hold your hands, full of love, up to Jesus in heaven or to Jesus in the Blessed Sacrament to give him your thanks.

Tell him, "Thank you, Jesus, for everything!"

Then tell Jesus some of the things you are thankful for.

Bonus activity after your prayer time:

In the days ahead, whenever something good happens or whenever something yucky happens, imagine gathering your love in your hands.

Then hold your hands, full of love, up to Jesus in heaven to give him your thanks.

18 Many psalms are beautiful prayers of thanksgiving and praise to God. Slowly, joyfully, and thoughtfully pray Psalm 100:

"Make a joyful noise to the LORD, all the lands!
  Serve the LORD with gladness!
  Come into his presence with singing!

Know that the LORD is God!
  It is he that made us, and we are his;
  we are his people, and the sheep of his pasture.

Enter his gates with thanksgiving,
  and his courts with praise!
  Give thanks to him, bless his name!

For the LORD is good;
  his mercy endures for ever,
  and his faithfulness to all generations."

**Now reread Psalm 100 as you
act out the psalm in your mind.**

Imagine making a joyful noise to God. What does it sound like?

Imagine serving him while singing him a song of gladness.

Imagine being a sheep with Jesus as your shepherd.

Imagine entering the gates of heaven, looking at God and saying,
"Thank you, God! I bless your name, God!"

Think of God loving your great-great-grandparents, loving
your great-grandparents, loving your grandparents, loving
your parents, loving you, loving your children, loving your
grandchildren, and on and on …

19   Ponder 1 Thessalonians 5:16–17:

"Rejoice always, pray constantly, give thanks in all circumstances; for this is the will of God in Christ Jesus for you."

Now slowly, joyfully, and thoughtfully pray,

Jesus, I rejoice and give thanks to you always! With your help, I will find reasons to thank you in all the moments of my life.

Take some time now to thank Jesus for as many things as you can think of.

20   Slowly, joyfully, and thoughtfully pray:

For my mother, father, and family,
I thank you, Jesus.

For making me a child of God in Baptism,
I thank you, Jesus.

For letting me belong to your holy Catholic Church,
I thank you, Jesus.

For all the graces you have given me
to help me love and serve you,
I thank you, Jesus.

For all the good things you have
given me during my entire life,
I thank you, Jesus.

For the promise of heaven after this life,
I thank you, Jesus.

WHAT ARE ASKING JESUS PRAYERS?

When you want your friend's help to do something or to solve a problem, you ask for help. When you share your worries with a friend hoping they can make you feel better, you are asking for help.

When we ask our Divine Friend for help, we are praying **asking Jesus prayers.**

There are two types of **asking Jesus prayers:** petitions and intercessions.

Petitions
are when you ask Jesus for his help for yourself.

Intercessions
are when you ask Jesus for help for someone else.

You can tell Jesus about your worries, your sadness, your hurts, your friends, and your loved ones.

His answers may not always be what you expect, but his answers are always full of love and help.

WORDS TO KNOW

PONDER: think and consider prayerfully

INTENTIONS: the requests you make to God

PETITIONS: when you ask Jesus for his help for yourself

INTERCESSIONS: when you ask Jesus for help for someone else

VENIAL SIN: a lesser offense against God or a sin not committed with full understanding

ASKING JESUS

Prayer Possibilities

1 Read and ponder:
Jesus says in the Gospel of Matthew,

"Ask, and it will be given you; seek, and you will find; knock, and it will be opened to you. For every one who asks receives, and he who seeks finds, and to him who knocks it will be opened" (Matthew 7:7–8).

With your eyes closed, imagine walking up to a beautiful door. You raise your hand and knock.

The door is opened by Jesus right away.

He looks at you and smiles. You feel deep peace and love as you look back at him.

As you imagine looking at Jesus in the doorway, ask him for any help that you might need for yourself or for someone else.

Bonus activity after your prayer time:

If you have a prayer request, give a quiet knock on a door, wall, desk, or something else to remind you of this Scripture verse. Then ask Jesus your prayer request.

2 JOURNAL ENTRY:

Ponder Matthew 7:7–8:

> **"Ask, and it will be given you; seek, and you will find; knock, and it will be opened to you. For every one who asks receives, and he who seeks finds, and to him who knocks it will be opened."**

Take some time to write your prayer requests in your journal.

3 JOURNAL ENTRY:

In your journal, make a petition and intercession web like the one below.

Write "**Jesus, please help**" in the center, and then write your petitions and intercessions in bubbles coming off the center.

4 Close your eyes. Picture Jesus' hands reaching out to you from heaven.

He is willing to help carry any sadness, worry, or burden that you feel.

As you touch your heart, imagine taking your worries, sadness, intentions, or petitions one by one from your heart. Then reach out as you place that prayer in Jesus' hands.

Tell Jesus,

Lord, I give you my worries and my intentions and place them in your hands.

Bonus activity after your prayer time:

When you start to worry too much, close your eyes and picture Jesus' hands reaching down from heaven to carry your worry. Place your worries in his hands.

5 Ponder how a sponge can hold a lot of water.

That water can then be squeezed out somewhere else. And sometimes the sponge has so much water in it, it drips as you carry it.

Closing your eyes, imagine that you are a sponge. But instead of soaking up water, you soak up lots and lots of Jesus' love. So much love that you drip his love everywhere you go and on everyone you pass. You could even squeeze Jesus' love on someone else who might be "dry," sad, or in trouble.

Slowly and thoughtfully pray:

Let me be a sponge, Lord, to soak up your love so I can squeeze it out on others.

Bonus activity after your prayer time:

Next time you see someone who is "dry," sad, or in trouble, imagine squeezing some of Jesus' love on them.

If you have any other prayer requests, take a moment to ask Jesus for his help.

115

6

When people die with venial sins, they might go to purgatory first before heaven.

Souls in purgatory are cleaned from their sin so they can stand fully in the light of God.

Our prayers can help clean these souls so they can go to their eternal happiness in heaven.

Think about the people who have died—those you love, those you know, and those you might not know.

Slowly and thoughtfully pray this prayer to help souls move from purgatory to heaven:

St. Gertrude the Great Prayer

"Eternal Father, I offer thee the most precious blood of thy divine Son, Jesus, in union with the Masses said throughout the world today, for all the holy souls in purgatory, for all sinners everywhere, for sinners in the universal church, those in my own home and within my family. Amen."

Bonus activity after your prayer time:

Talk to your parents about how you are praying for the souls in purgatory. Say the St. Gertrude the Great Prayer with them to help more souls go to heaven.

If you have any other prayer requests, take a moment to ask Jesus for his help.

7 When two objects are connected by a string, they stay close together.

Closing your eyes, imagine your heart connected to Jesus' Sacred Heart with an unbreakable string.

(If you are in church or in Adoration, you can look at Jesus in the Blessed Sacrament while you imagine this string.)

This unbreakable string keeps you close to Jesus.

If you start to make bad choices that lead you away from Jesus toward sin or if you get lost with what choice to make, **Jesus can pull you back to his heart if you allow him to.**

If you ask Jesus to keep you connected to him, he can gently pull the string to bring you back to him and good choices.

Slowly and thoughtfully pray:

Lord, connect my heart to your Sacred Heart with an unbreakable string so that if I go astray or get lost you can pull me back to your heart. Please let me never stray from you. Please help me stay close and always connected to you.

Optional journal entry:

Draw a picture in your journal of your heart connected to Jesus' heart with an unbreakable string.

If you have any other prayer requests, take a moment to ask Jesus for his help.

8 Ask Jesus for one of the seven gifts of the Holy Spirit to help you live a better life:[20]

Wisdom
Wisdom gives you a love "for the things of God" and helps to guide your "whole life and all … [your] actions to His honor and glory."

Understanding
Understanding allows you "to know more clearly the mysteries of faith."

Counsel
Counsel allows you "to see and choose correctly what will" give most glory to God and help you get to heaven.

Fortitude
Fortitude gives you courage "to do the will of God in all things."

Knowledge
Knowledge "points out to … [you] the path to follow and the dangers to avoid in order to reach heaven."

Piety
Piety helps you "love God as a Father, and obey Him because … [you] love Him.

Fear of the Lord
Fear of the Lord fills you with the highest respect for God and a strong dislike of offending him.

Or ask Jesus for one of the twelve fruits of the Holy Spirit:[21]

charity (love)	kindness	faithfulness
joy	goodness	modesty
peace	generosity	self-control
patience	gentleness	chastity

If you have any other prayer requests,
take a moment to ask Jesus for his help.

9 Slowly and thoughtfully pray and ponder:

"I want to be completely transformed into Your mercy and to be Your living reflection, O Lord. May the greatest of all divine attributes, that of Your unfathomable mercy, pass through my heart and soul to my neighbor.

Help me, O Lord, that my eyes may be merciful, so that I may never suspect or judge from appearances, but look for what is beautiful in my neighbors' souls and come to their rescue.

Help me, that my ears may be merciful, so that I may give heed [that is, pay attention] to my neighbors' needs and not be indifferent to their pains and moanings.

Help me, O Lord, that my tongue may be merciful, so that I should never speak negatively of my neighbor, but have a word of comfort and forgiveness for all.

Help me, O Lord, that my hands may be merciful and filled with good deeds, so that I may do only good to my neighbors and take upon myself the more difficult and toilsome tasks.

Help me, that my feet may be merciful, so that I may hurry to assist my neighbor, overcoming my own fatigue and weariness ...

Help me, O Lord, that my heart may be merciful so that I myself may feel all the sufferings of my neighbor ...
May Your mercy, O Lord, rest upon me."[22]

— St. Faustina

Bonus activity after your prayer time:

If you are having a hard time showing someone mercy with your eyes, ears, mouth, hands, feet, or heart, quietly touch that part of your body and say, "Help me, O Lord, to be merciful."

If you have any other prayer requests, take a moment to ask Jesus for his help.

10   Close your eyes and imagine someone giving you a gift.

Think about how much easier it is to receive that gift if you are near to the person giving it to you.

Now think about how hard it would be to receive that gift if the giver was standing far away from you.

Sin separates you from God.

The more sins you commit, the bigger your separation is from him.

Prayerfully ask Jesus,

Jesus, help cleanse me from my sin so I can be nearer and closer to you. Help me to receive the gift of your grace more easily.

Bonus activity after your prayer time:

On your way up to Communion at Mass, ask Jesus to cleanse you of your sin so you can be very near to him when you receive his Body. Ask him also to allow you to receive as much grace as you possibly can.

11 The adults who help lead your community, your country, and your world need your prayers. Take some time to call to mind the names of the people in each category below.

Ask Jesus to watch over and guide each one of these leaders and the decisions they make.

Pope
- Name the pope.

Bishops
- Name the bishops you know one by one.

Priests
- Name the priests you know one by one.

Deacons
- Name the deacons you know one by one.

Nuns
- Name the nuns you know one by one.

Teachers
- Name the teachers you know one by one.

Principals
- Name the principals you know one by one.

City and state leaders
- Name the city and state leaders you know one by one.

Presidents
- Name the presidents you know one by one.

World leaders
- Name the world leaders you know one by one.

Bonus activity after your prayer time:

When you see a leader in person or on the news, say a quick prayer asking Jesus to guide that person to make choices that are pleasing to God.

If you have any other prayer requests, take a moment to ask Jesus for his help.

12   Ponder how God sees things differently than you do.

You might look at a friend or stranger and think the person is angry, but God sees even deeper than you to see that sometimes the person isn't really angry but instead is worried or scared.

You might act differently toward a person you thought was angry if you realized that he or she was actually worried. You might act with more kindness toward a worried person.

If you look at people sitting by themselves, you might think they want to be left alone, but God sees that often those people feel all alone and could use a friend.

JOURNAL ENTRY:

Write in your journal and prayerfully say,

Let me see with your eyes, O Lord, not mine.

Draw a picture of how you might see something and then how God might see the very same thing.

If you have any other prayer requests, take a moment to ask Jesus for his help.

13 Ponder how warm and cozy you feel when you are wrapped up in a soft blanket.

Now think of people who might be feeling sad, sick, or in need of a little extra love.

Using each person's name, ask Jesus to wrap up that person in his love like a blanket:

Jesus, please wrap up _____ in your blanket of love.

Optional journal entry:

Draw a picture of someone that you know really needs God's help. Draw that person wrapped up in Jesus' blanket of love.

Bonus activity after your prayer time:

When you see or hear of someone who needs God's help, ask Jesus to wrap that person up in his blanket of love.

Next, using your imagination, picture that person wrapped up cozily by Jesus.

If you have any other prayer requests, take a moment to ask Jesus for his help.

14 With your eyes closed, breathe slowly and deeply. With each slow breath, say,

Lord Jesus, make me holy.

Do this ten times or even twenty times!

If you have any other prayer requests, take a moment to ask Jesus for his help.

Bonus activity after your prayer time:

When you first wake up in the morning, say, "Lord Jesus, make me holy today." If you would like, make and decorate a sign to place by your bed as a reminder.

15 Ponder what St. John Paul II said to a child preparing to receive first Holy Communion:

Jesus "is the greatest friend you will ever have ... Tell him your secrets. Tell him your joys and the things that make you sad. Tell him about the people whom you love ... Above all tell him how much you love him."[23]

Jesus is your Divine Friend, your friend from heaven, your friend who is God.

Daily, even hourly, Jesus is waiting for you, waiting to hear from you, waiting to be asked to be part of your day, waiting to share your burdens, *waiting to give you his love.*

Take a few minutes to tell Jesus about your secrets, about your joys and sorrows, and about the people you love.

Share your heart—share the way you hold and feel love—with Jesus.

Close your eyes now and know that Jesus is here with you this very second. Even if you can't feel it, his love warmly and wonderfully surrounds you.

16 Slowly and thoughtfully pray this prayer:

Offering and Prayer of St. Ignatius Loyola

"Take, Lord, and receive all my liberty, my memory, my understanding, and my entire will, all I have and call my own. You have given all to me. To you, Lord, I return it. Everything is yours; do with it what you will. Give me only your love and your grace; that is enough for me."

If you have any other prayer requests, take a moment to ask Jesus for his help.

17

Slowly and thoughtfully pray:

St. Augustine's Prayer to the Holy Spirit

"Breathe in me, O Holy Spirit, that all my thoughts may be holy. Act in me, O Holy Spirit, that my work, too, may be holy.

Draw my heart, O Holy Spirit, that I may love only what is holy. Strengthen me, O Holy Spirit, to defend all that is holy.

Guard me, then, O Holy Spirit, that I always may be holy. Amen."

If you have any other prayer requests, take a moment to ask Jesus for his help.

18 Slowly and thoughtfully pray:

Prayer of St. Francis

"Lord, make me an instrument of your peace:
where there is hatred, let me sow love;
where there is injury, pardon;
where there is doubt, faith;
where there is despair, hope;
where there is darkness, light;
where there is sadness, joy.

O divine Master, grant that I may not so much seek
to be consoled as to console,
to be understood as to understand,
to be loved as to love.
For it is in giving that we receive,
it is in pardoning that we are pardoned,
and it is in dying that we are born to eternal life.
Amen."

If you have any other prayer requests,
take a moment to ask Jesus for his help.

19

Jesus talks about the *corporal works of mercy* in the Gospel of Matthew. They are "a model for how we should treat all others, as if they were Christ in disguise."[24] (A disguise is a costume that makes someone hard to recognize.)

To visit prisoners is one of the seven corporal works of mercy.

"People in prison are still people, made in the image and likeness of God. No matter what someone has done, they deserve the opportunity to hear the Word of God and find the Truth of the message of Christ."[25]

Ask Jesus to help prisoners be sorry for the wrong things they have done and to know the truth that he is their Savior and he loves them.

You may be too young to visit people in prison; however, you can certainly pray for them.

Bonus activity after your prayer time:

Find the names of all seven corporal works of mercy. Consider what you can do to perform one or more corporal works of mercy in the coming days.

20 Slowly and thoughtfully pray:

Student's Prayer
(based on a prayer by St. Thomas Aquinas)

Come, Holy Spirit, divine Creator, true source of light and fountain of wisdom! Pour your wisdom upon me when I don't understand things. Chase away the darkness of sin, too. Grant me a quick mind to understand, a strong memory, a good and easy plan in learning, the ability to understand, and a clear way of expressing myself. Guide the beginning of my work, direct its progress, and bring it to a successful finish. This I ask through Jesus Christ, true God and true man, living and reigning with you and the Father, forever and ever. Amen.[26]

Ask Jesus to help you with any struggles you are having at school.

If you have any other prayer requests,
take a moment to ask Jesus for his help.

Bonus activity after your prayer time:

Before a test at school, in your mind quietly ask
Jesus for a quick mind to understand the material
and a strong memory to know the right answers.

BEFORE YOU GO

Have you listened to Jesus?

1. You don't want to miss anything Jesus wants to tell you.

2. Turn to the gray **"How Do I Listen to Jesus?"** section for help.

3. Spend a few minutes listening.

Have you said your goodbyes to Jesus?

1. Say goodbye to Jesus just like you say goodbye when you leave an earthly friend.

2. Invite Jesus to stay in your heart after your prayer time.

Jesus' love for you is enormous. It is bottomless.

He is always with you: when you are praying, in church, when you are scared, when you are happy, when you are playing … always!

Do you have more time to spend with Jesus?

If so, turn the page to the orange "Pray More" section.

PRAY MORE

EUCHARISTIC ADORATION

There is a certain joy in being face-to-face with an earthly friend, sitting in the same room together. You get excited when you know that opportunity is coming. You might even count the days or hours until you get together.

Eucharistic Adoration is very special because you are getting together with Jesus.

You are sitting in the very same room with Jesus, the King of all creation, the Lord of Lords, your Savior, God! You are face-to-face with your Divine Friend, Jesus.

St. Teresa of Calcutta said, "Every holy hour we make so pleases the Heart of Jesus that it will be recorded in Heaven and retold for all eternity."[27]

Jesus waits for YOU to come spend time with him in the Eucharist.

When you visit Jesus in Adoration, he pours out graces, blessings, love, and peace into your soul.

Take some time to visit Jesus in Eucharistic Adoration. You might count the days, hours, minutes until you can see Jesus, THE most amazing friend you could ever have, face-to-face.

WHAT IS EUCHARISTIC ADORATION?

Eucharistic Adoration is when Jesus, in the form of the Eucharist, is placed in a clear window inside a *monstrance* (a golden holder for the Eucharist).

The monstrance is placed on the altar for everyone to see, love, and adore Jesus.

Jesus is present under the appearance of bread, called a Host, which was consecrated during Mass.

The Host usually looks like a white circle.

Consecration means the priest, with the power of the Holy Spirit, changes ordinary bread into the Body, Blood, Soul, and Divinity of Jesus.

Jesus is every bit as real in the Eucharist as when he walked with his disciples two thousand years ago.

Jesus is just as real as when he laid his hands on the children and blessed them. (You can read about that in the Bible in Matthew 19:13–15.)

Jesus just looks like bread, but his real Body, Blood, Soul, and Divinity is ABSOLUTELY present.

He is truly there under the appearance of bread.

During Eucharistic Adoration, you spend time talking to Jesus and listening to him.

You look at Jesus, and he looks at you.

You know Jesus loves you, and you love him in return.

WHAT SHOULD I DO IN ADORATION?

Some ways to pray in Adoration are

- all of the four kinds of prayer possibilities in this book
- traditional Catholic prayers
- the Chaplet of Divine Mercy
- the Rosary

POLITE ADORATION BEHAVIOR

Since you will be in front of the actual presence of God, you want to show Jesus respect and honor:

- Enter and leave the Adoration chapel quietly.

- Genuflect on both knees when you enter and leave your pew. Be sure to look at Jesus in the Blessed Sacrament and slowly make the Sign of the Cross while genuflecting.

- Kneel in your pew for a few minutes when you first enter. This shows Jesus your respect and love.

- You can sit or kneel during your prayer time. Use good posture.

- You can bow your head, close your eyes, or look at Jesus in the Blessed Sacrament.

- Give Jesus your full attention!

- Don't stare around the chapel. Don't wander around the chapel.

- Do all your personal praying in the quiet of your heart.

- If you are taking part in a group Adoration, be sure to participate aloud in any group prayers especially during Exposition, Divine Praises, and Benediction.

- Invite Jesus to stay with you when you leave Adoration.

TRADITIONAL PRAYERS

You talk to your earthly friends to compliment them, apologize to them, thank them, or ask them for help. You also share your thoughts, feelings, and beliefs with friends. Many times, you talk to your friends in a combination of these ways in a single visit.

Prayer time with your Divine Friend is very similar. You can use a combination of the four basic ways to pray: praise, **being sorry**, thanksgiving, and asking Jesus.

Plus, you can share with Jesus your thoughts, feelings, and beliefs. All combinations of prayer to Jesus are ways to build a stronger friendship with your Divine Friend.

Look at the traditional Catholic prayers that follow to see the different ways you can talk to Jesus by using these prayers.

Then take some time to slowly and prayerfully say the words of each prayer.

OUR FATHER

Our Father, who art in heaven, hallowed be thy name; thy kingdom come, thy will be done, on earth as it is in heaven. Give us this day our daily bread, and forgive us our trespasses as we forgive those who trespass against us; and lead us not into temptation, but deliver us from evil. Amen.

HAIL MARY

Hail Mary, full of grace, the Lord is with thee. Blessed art thou among women, and blessed is the fruit of thy womb, Jesus. Holy Mary, Mother of God, pray for us sinners, now and at the hour of our death. Amen.

GLORY BE

Glory be to the Father, and to the Son, and to the Holy Spirit, as it was in the beginning, is now, and ever shall be, world without end. Amen.

APOSTLES' CREED

I believe in God, the Father almighty, Creator of heaven and earth, and in Jesus Christ, his only Son, our Lord, who was conceived by the Holy Spirit, born of the Virgin Mary, suffered under Pontius Pilate, was crucified, died and was buried; he descended to hell; on the third day he rose again from the dead; he ascended into heaven, and is seated at the right hand of God the Father almighty; from there he will come to judge the living and the dead. I believe in the Holy Spirit, the holy catholic Church, the communion of saints, the forgiveness of sins, the resurrection of the body, and life everlasting. Amen.

THE ROSARY

Say either a single decade or the whole Rosary. Use your fingers or a set of rosary beads to count off the prayers.

Choose from:

The Joyful Mysteries
(usually prayed on Mondays and Saturdays)

1. The Annunciation
2. The Visitation
3. The Nativity
4. The Presentation
5. The Finding of Jesus in the Temple

The Glorious Mysteries
(usually prayed on Wednesdays and Saturdays)

1. The Resurrection
2. The Ascension
3. The Descent of the Holy Spirit
4. The Assumption of Mary
5. The Coronation of Mary

The Sorrowful Mysteries
(usually prayed on Tuesdays and Fridays)

1. The Agony in the Garden
2. The Scourging at the Pillar
3. The Crowning with Thorns
4. The Carrying of the Cross
5. The Crucifixion

The Luminous Mysteries
(usually prayed on Thursdays)

1. The Baptism of Jesus
2. The Wedding at Cana
3. The Proclamation of the Kingdom
4. The Transfiguration
5. The Institution of the Eucharist

THIS IS HOW TO PRAY A DECADE OF THE ROSARY

- Make the Sign of the Cross
- On the large bead, say one Our Father.
- Say ten Hail Marys using the smaller beads.
- As you pray the decade of your choosing, ponder that mystery.
- Pray one Glory Be. End by praying, "O my Jesus, forgive us our sins, save us from the fires of hell, and lead all souls to heaven, especially those in most need of thy mercy."

To pray the whole Rosary, begin with the Sign of the Cross, then pray the Apostles' Creed, one Our Father, three Hail Marys, and one Glory Be. Then pray all five decades in a set of mysteries, pondering the mysteries. Pray the Hail, Holy Queen Prayer. Look up how to pray the Rosary to find the words to the Rosary's closing prayer, too.

It will take about twenty minutes to pray the whole Rosary.

HAIL, HOLY QUEEN

Hail, Holy Queen, Mother of mercy, our life, our sweetness, and our hope. To thee do we cry, poor banished children of Eve; to thee do we send up our sighs, mourning and weeping in this valley of tears. Turn, then, most gracious advocate, thine eyes of mercy toward us, and after this, our exile, show unto us the blessed fruit of thy womb, Jesus. O clement, O loving, O sweet Virgin Mary.

THE DIVINE MERCY CHAPLET

Use a set of rosary beads (or your fingers) to count off the prayers.

The chaplet begins with the Sign of the Cross, then one Our Father, one Hail Mary, and the Apostles' Creed.

On the large beads (the Our Father beads), say the "Eternal Father" prayer:

Eternal Father, I offer you the Body and Blood, Soul and Divinity of your dearly beloved Son, our Lord Jesus Christ, in atonement for our sins and those of the whole world.

On each of the small beads (the Hail Mary beads), say the "For the Sake of His Sorrowful Passion" prayer:

For the sake of his sorrowful passion, have mercy on us and on the whole world.

Conclude with the "Holy God" prayer three times:

Holy God, Holy Mighty One, Holy Immortal One, have mercy on us and on the whole world.

Bonus activity after your prayer time:

Three o'clock in the afternoon is called the hour of mercy. It is the time when Jesus died on the Cross. Say the Divine Mercy Chaplet at three o'clock one afternoon. If you would like, set an alarm to remind you to pray.

NOTES

1. See homily of St. John Paul II for the Solemnity of the Body and Blood of Christ (June 14, 1979), vatican.va.

2. See homily of St. John Paul II for the Solemnity of the Body and Blood of Christ (June 14, 1979), vatican.va.

3. Homily of St. John Paul II in San Antonio, Texas, Sunday, September 13, 1987, vatican.va.

4. "Prayer in Praise of God, St. Francis of Assisi," in *Spirit of Truth: Living as a Disciple of Christ Student Workbook* (Sophia Institute for Teachers, 2017), 47, books.google.com.

5. Based on St. John Paul II, *Reconciliation and Penance* (December 2, 1984), 31.III, vatican.va: "The essential act of penance, on the part of the penitent, is contrition, a clear and decisive rejection of the sin committed, together with a resolution not to commit it again, out of the love which one has for God and which is reborn with repentance."

6. From St. John Bosco, *Life of Dominic Savio, Pupil at the Oratory of St. Francis de Sales.*

7. Pope Francis, "The Grace of Being Ashamed," morning meditation (October 25, 2013), vatican.va.

8. Pope Francis, "The Tangibility and Simplicity of the Small," homily (April 29, 2020), vatican.va.

9. Pope Francis, "Return to God and Return to the Embrace of the Father," homily (March 20, 2020), vatican.va.

10. St. John Paul II, homily in San Antonio, Texas (September 13, 1987), vatican.va (formatting altered).

11. From Pope Francis, "Examination of Conscience," morning meditation (September 4, 2018), vatican.va.

12. The following questions are taken from "24 Hours for the Lord," St. Michael Church (website), March 4, 2016, stmichaelcranford.org, based on Pope Francis' booklet "Safeguard Your Heart," February 22, 2015. Modified for children by the author.

13. "In the life of the body a man is sometimes sick, and unless he take medicine, he will die: even so in the spiritual life a man is sick on account of sin; wherefore he needs medicine so that he may be restored to health; and this grace is bestowed in the sacrament of Penance" (St. Thomas Aquinas, "Exposition of the Apostles' Creed," 10, quoted in John A. Hardon, S.J., ed., *The Treasury of Catholic Wisdom* [San Francisco: Ignatius, 1995], 291).

14. Pope Francis, Angelus address (February 16, 2014), vatican.va.

15. St. John Paul II, homily in San Antonio, Texas (September 13, 1987), vatican.va.

16. St. John Vianney, "On Temptations (C.)," quoted in *Thoughts of the Curé of Ars* (Ravenio Books, 2015), e-book.

17. Source unknown; sometimes attributed to St. Ambrose.

18. Based on St. Gertrude the Great, *The Revelations of St. Gertrude* 23. Modified for children by the author.

19. St. Josemaria Escriva, *The Way* 268.

20. Definitions for wisdom, understanding, fortitude, and piety are taken from *Baltimore Catechism* #3 (1891), lesson 16, questions 701, 703, 706–707, baltimore-catechism.com. Definitions for counsel, knowledge, and fear of the Lord are taken from Jacques Forget, "Holy Ghost," in *The Catholic Encyclopedia*, vol. 7 (New York: Robert Appleton Company, 1910), newadvent.org. See also *Catechism of the Catholic Church* 1831.

21. See *Catechism of the Catholic Church* 1832.

22. St. Faustina, *Diary of Saint Maria Faustina Kowalska* 163, quoted in "Prayer to Be Merciful to Others," The Divine Mercy (website), accessed June 20, 2022, thedivinemercy.org/message/spirituality/prayer.

23. John Paul II, address to students from the "Katherine School of the Air," Melbourne, Australia, November 29, 1986.

24. "The Corporal Works of Mercy," United States Conference of Catholic Bishops (website), accessed June 20, 2022, usccb.org.

25. "The Corporal Works of Mercy," usccb.org.

26. Based on "A Student's Prayer (by St. Thomas Aquinas)," accessed June 20, 2022, catholic.org. Modified for children by the author.

27. Quoted in Sr. JosephMary f.t.i., "St. Teresa of Calcutta: A Reflection on Eucharistic Adoration," Ave Maria Meditations, September 5, 2017, airmaria.com.

Ascension
PO Box 1990
West Chester, PA 19380
1-800-376-0520
ascensionpress.com

Cover design: Lily Fitzgibbons

Printed in USA

22 23 24 25 26 5 4 3 2 1

ISBN 978-1-954881-79-2